SHALOM, MY TEARDROP!

MIMOZA EREBARA

Translated from the Albanian by Arben P. Latifi

Červená Barva Press
Somerville, Massachusetts

Červená Barva Press
P.O. Box 440357
W. Somerville, MA 02144-3222

www.cervenabarvapress.com
Bookstore: www.thelostbookshelf.com

Cover Art: Wailing Wall by Gustav Bauernfeind (1848-1904)

Cover design: William J. Kelle

ISBN: 978-1-950063-27-7

ACKNOWLEDGMENTS

I thank my parents for all the boundless love they have given me, my place whose roots hold me tight.

TABLE OF CONTENTS

SHALOM, MY TEARDROP!

SHALOM, MY TEARDROP!

This land, even though far away,
won't let me go...

With her love,
hidden somewhere
in the depths of my sinews,
which freshened up in a different air,
despite the dazzling spears
of negation,
that pierce me through
like slander.

A single leaf of fire
holds me onto the marrow of nonoblivion,
like a teardrop
that never dropped down...

IN FRONT OF DAVID'S GATE

With Your Gate upon my shoulders,
I roam the world.

Like in a jigsaw puzzle,
I try to install it
In hollows of states,
In hollows of peace,
Feverishly, chimingly,
Like mists void of a memory
Of Nations.
Yet, it won't fit in,
And I have to return
Back to where I started from –
A traveler without a trail.

With Your Gate upon my shoulders,
I reach in front of the Ancient Walls,
And right there,
I easily plant it on.

IN JERUSALEM I CRAVE TO BE

There,
The old olive tree
Never dries up,
When its trunk brimming with life is hewn
By sharp-edged rocks,
Hot iron,
And wild weather,

There,
Where cobblestones talk to me
Through breath,
Like in the early childhood game,
And create
Mosaics of Life,

There,
Where Time stops
In its Prospectiveness,

There,
In its air,
Where a whimsical,
Expansionistic
Cell of my leafy body
Witnesses the moon's greed
Gobbling up shelters, gardens, and the dogs' barking,
Where lips turn into victims of passions
Eternally...

There,
In Jerusalem,
I crave to be.

KOTEL MA'ARAVI
At the Wailing Wall, Jerusalem

Powerless to stop it,
I have let so much blood to bleed
In the violence-impregnated day-nights,
There, in the Old City,
Where broken
Peace
Passes by idifferent, yet in stubborn pride -
A swallow in the air,
Undried sweat
Of our warm breaths,
For the souls...
In the hope that one day,
Kotel Ma'aravi
Receives my prayer
By the stones,
Where daggers slay the faith,
Whilst air caresses every whiff of respiration...
There it will be, awaiting
To tell me
The secret to Survival.

Right there, I'll be expecting for my prayer
To commence its journey...

HaKotel HaMa'ravi [Hebr.] - *A part of the Western Wall, also
known as the "Wailing Wall", where Jewish people traditionally
pray in grief for the destruction of Temple Mount first by the
Babylonians and later on by the Romans.*

DEAD SEA, SALTY SEA

I plunged into the Dead Sea
To see
How dead it was,
But I got stuck in there,
With its salt
Tanning my skin.

HA-SHOAH*
In Yad Vashem, the Museum of Holocaust Victims

Like in a crematorium,
Inside me burn
Grain, Bone, Light, Breath.
Everything is extinguished
In the ashes of existence,
Which gained its very soul from air...
I want to leave,
But I am pinned there,
Petrified,
Like a black pigeon,
In the hollow sockets
Of those beautiful eyes – once,
When they'd breathe life toward Life.
I pause
To find the akin to myself
In the field, where the wheat is freshly cropped...

And here's where I am,
Me
Along with a wheat-ear of memory
That, twixt smoke and ashes -
poor rosy smoke -
Confides to me in ecstatic whisper:
My, wasn't Hope so beautiful
Under winglets of butterflies
Dripping with dew!

*Ha-Shoah [Hebr.] - *Commemoration*

8

AT ARAD

The sky is burning with my longing
And on airish particles
It flies, far and beyond...
Towards the sands
And the desert rock,
Which is burning with the breath
That is roasting me,
While I strip even the last ember
For you,
My rock
Of the golden night...
This star
Comes to my dream
Like a lost soul,
Like a tale yet unheard.
Desert –
The craddle
Of my breath.

I HAVE A TEMPLE, THIS IS ALL I NEED

With fate in my arms,
I am departing
Towards the Signs
To find out The Enigma,
The Mystery,
The Magic of the Earth,
Which awakens me,
Upsets me,
And, in screaming silence,
Sings to me
About
My gene
Lost through the pranks of Time.
I am heading there,
Where the dead
Have more to tell than those alive:
To my Land,
So that
They show me the trail.
– Shalom!

Shalom [Hebr.] - *Peace*

FALL IN TEL-AVIV

The sea dressed up
In rain colors
And took a look at itself
On the mirror of the blue sky.
Didn't like it:
Too blue,
Too beautiful,
Painfully beautiful.

Its appearance resembled life
In dreams.

Hence, it undid that look
And dressed in a grey drizzle
The roofs
And my eyelids

In the blue Tel-Aviv.

THE WOMEN OF ASHDOD

Silent
Like the first petal,
Like wings at flight,
They walk
Softly in pride,
Rulers,
Temptors
Of Peace,
As proclaimed by the first sunray at dawn.

While to the shining pupils
Of their boisterous
Children
They pledge
Everything else they have.

PROPHECIES
In Galilee

I am bathing in prophecies.
The sunny water, however,
Mounts up
And covers me altogether.
I am no longer awash
Solely in My own Prophecy.
There are
Thousands of them around
Belonging to no certain face or age,
For they gifted their eyes to Me,
So that I can make out
What the Prophecies foretell.

And I keep silent, because
Silence
Is what the moment calls for.

SUNSET IN ISRAEL

The sun set over Tel-Aviv.
The old fisherman's shadow faded in the dusk,
By the blue sea.
In the dusk faded the buildings.
Falafel around the corner ran out for today as well.
Flowers discreetly covered themselves.
The young lady soldiers let their hair loose,
Like dreams, to flow down their shoulders.
The camels, like sphinxes, lay down in silence,
With the lonely desert talking to them
In a myserious language, under an undecipherable,
Thousand-year old rite,
And the Bedouin faded inside his eyes of longing,
And the babies went to their peaceful sleep.
The Noah's ark didn't depart on this sunset either.
The rock discharged its entire heat in the air.
Libraries, museums, all closed doors.
Cheerfulness, nonetheless, dressed up half-lightish, half-
    nightish,
Went out in the streets, free, untethered, dazzling -
The cheerfulness over Ashdod
And over Arad.
Masada had of long concealed her wounds
And cheered at cheerfulness.
The Wailing Wall beckoned Hope nearby.

The sun set
Over My rough Land,
And so did
My soft teardrop...

IDENTITY

We were born under trees,
Would grow up around trees,
Would die hung up in trees.
We WERE trees —
No roots,
But bare trunks,
No leaves,
But fruits.

We were
A breed of dry sticks,
Shooting up from beneath the roots
And perishing up above on a branch,
Where the fingers,
Like stubborn-headed worms,
Would eat
The last leaves in fall.

LIPS ABANDONED TO LONELINESS

In this narrow street,
full of shadows of fluttering clouds
and domes,
the lips are running at random,
trying to leave, leave, nothing but leave
toward the chiaroscuro depths
of a stoical spirit;
to cuddle for a short while,
long enough to rest a bit,
to then launch their unstoppable assault
of never-ending bittersweetness.

Ah, for the lips that -
in this narrow street
of domes
and fluttering clouds -
were abandoned to loneliness!

MY EGO IN THE 3rd PERSON

It gets lost amid the abstract sounds
In search of My Ego in the 1st Person,
Under the lymph of conflicts,
Cromosomes,
Galaxies,
Which revolve
In larval gawking
At the existential risk.
Stop!
You Ego of Mine in the 3rd Person!
Stay put at your own home –
My Ego in the 1st Person –
And listen up
To the soundlessness,
To the clouds,
And to the rocks of silence!
My Ego in the 3rd Person,
Perfidious you are,
In your persistence to chase
Idiotic flirting affairs,
Like worthless eggshells
Thrown into the garbage bin!
Go to the life you're looking for,
My Ego in the 3rd Person,
Holding
Hand-in-hand and lip-to-lip
With My Ego in the 1st Person!
You are inviting me
To burn
Under groundless roots.
However, I won't move!

The Earth's Gravity takes me
Toward my amebic,
One-celled self.
I won't stay because I cannot stay!
My Ego in the 1st Person won't let me to.
It pulls me unceasingly towards
The reverberating clouds
And the tempting pollen,
Like the budding lust
Of My joint Egos.

THE LAMPSHADE

I'm merely a lampshade,
staying silent
in a corner of the bedroom.
Had I a tongue,
I would tell...
Ah, what I would tell!

AT BEN GURION AIRPORT, TEL-AVIV

Oh, how this warm air
Envelops the whole of me,
All the way through to my bones,
For centuries frozen
By icy winds
And frosty blasts,
Away from my own Land,
For centuries blown
Who knows where!

Oh, how this warm air
Gurgles through my veins,
Down to my remotest cell,
And pumps life into me!
I open my chest
And take refuge in the depths
Of my longing,
Originating from centuries –
Who knows whence!

August 27, 1997

RACHEL

Up to the yellow line runs Rachel,
With her blue-grey eyes,
Which the Russians disliked.
Up to the yellow line and no further,
With her blue-grey eyes weeping
In the eyes of the absconder, stumped
At a nonplus about what he's doing.
Poor Rachel runs
Like sun in its last days.
She runs
Aware that she'll nevermore see
Those nonplused eyes of her sweetheart.
With her blue-grey eyes in tears,
She runs
Up to the yellow line.

IN THE GRAVEYARD
Tel-Aviv

I visited the graveyard
And the dead spoke to me.
They recognized me,
Being all one and the same,
(Me having always voted for the King-Tree)
Except that,
Along centuries, they had burnt out in deserts
And left behind but simple stone slates
For me to touch on
And decode.

CREPUSCULE
Beer-Sheva

I am going to leave, one day, I know;
So soon, alas, it was never my wish.
I gave him nought, he gave me nought;
We but lingered on the same bridge.

DON'T WASH MY TROUSERS, WOMAN...

Don't wash my dirty trousers,
Kind, unknown woman,
Leave them as they are, all soil and dust,
And shed you no tears...

Don't wash my dirty trousers,
Kind sister,
Leave them as they are, all soil and dust,
For this soil is but what's left of my Land...

Don't wash my dirty trousers,
Kind soul,
Leave them as they are, all soil and dust,
For, one day, with this soil I'll cover
My poor child...

KNESSET, IN FRONT OF ME

I admire the birds' chant,
When weeping for the lost sunray,
Or singing to the displaced.
I adore it;
My palate goes dry, my saliva halts,
While I listen,
I solely listen
To the tunes in centuries unaltered.
I admire that chant,
And the birds more so -
When not in a cage!

Knesset [Hebr.] – *the Israeli Parliament*

A THREE-ANGLED NUDE ON
KRISTALLNACHT

My round,
Innocent
Being
Tosses halfway in bed.
My being,
Without you,
In this
Brutally
Broken night.

The Globe,
That carries my being and you,
Tosses halfway in space.
Smashed in shards is the Globe,
Without you,
Smashed in shards is my mind.

I cannot toss any more;
The shards drive deep down my skin
And the blood bleeds.
They clutched you away, my dear,
Pushed you against the window...
Your blood covered me,
The shards of glass and a crown of white flowers.
My life stopped halfway,
Without you.

MY FATHERLAND...?!

I run like mad by the seashore,
Climb up the mountains of waves,
And desperately
Seek
My Fatherland
In every tree,
In every leaf of grass...
I seek
For my idol,
My child and dad,
My mom and rocky plods,
The white *kippas*,
The guns hanging on the wall...
I pat them gently with quivering fingers
And scream out
To the point of such reverberation
As could set my chest ablast.
I am never tired of looking, again and again,
For that beautiful one of mine -
My Fatherland.

I know it is there...

THE RAIN ON THE OTHER SIDE OF JERUSALEM

Souls are falling like rain,
Soaking the dome of the mosque,
Soaking the folks, breath to breath,
Under grey clouds.
Wrathy are the souls and hurl rains
And sweat to turn everything into ashes,
Whereas we, the living souls,
Come out and soak under the rains,
Whereas the souls of the dead enter within us,
And we shelter them
Under grey clouds.

ABOUT THE AUTHOR

Mimoza Erebara, Jewish / Albanian, was born in Tirana, Albania. She is the author of the following books: "To Accompany a Hope" (poetry), "Cry of Love" (poetry), "Adventures of 10x10 and the Upside Down Munuriro" (Fairy Tale), "Wrongly in Love" (Stories), "Torn Reason" (poetry), "Symbrapshti" (fairy tale), "Dry Rent" (stories), "Peace without a Prophet" (poetry), "He and She: Love Messages" (poetry), "Shalom , My Tears" (poetry), " Spirit in the Desert" (poetry), "Philosophy in Metaphor" (literary studies and criticism), and Anthology of Hebrew Poetry. Mimoza has been published in numerous literary magazines in Albania and abroad. She has received "Gold Medals" for poetry from the European Academy of Arts, Paris, France, and many awards in the country. She holds the title of "Ambassador of Peace." Mimoza works as a journalist in the daily press in Tirana and is editor of many volumes.

ABOUT THE TRANSLATOR

Arben P. Latifi graduated in English Studies from the State University of Tirana, Albania [1985]. As an Albanian and US citizen, he is passionate about traveling, world culture, and literature. He has taught English in Albania, USA, Oman, and China. Currently Arben settled back in his native Albania. His Albanian-English, English-Albanian translations, mostly poetry and history, reflects accuracy and faithfulness to the original text, while enhancing its merits through elements such as cohesion, imagery, vocabulary, and musicality. Arben is fluent in English, Albanian, Italian, Greek, and Russian.

www.ingramcontent.com/pod-product-compliance
Lightning Source LLC
Chambersburg PA
CBHW020954030426
42339CB00004B/92